Collins

THE ICE

ALAN PARKINSON

Contents

Found in the snow and ice	2
What happens next?	6
Studying the Ice Man	10
Ötzi's last day…	28
An icy grave	32
Mountain scenery	36
More bodies	40
So what of Ötzi now?	46
CSI Ötzi	52

Found in the snow and ice

On a bright and sunny day in September 1991, two German tourists are hiking in the Alps. The mountain Erika and Helmut Simon are climbing is ten thousand feet high. They stop to take some amazing photos near the summit.

It is just after lunchtime. In a hurry to get back to their car, they take a short cut down the mountainside. They leave the main path and pick their way down a steep, stony gully, at the side of a section of ice.

The gully is full of drifts of snow. Helmut notices something brown against the whiteness of the snow. He thinks it might be litter. He carefully climbs down to take a closer look, before turning to his wife. "I think we've found a dead body," he says.

The body has skin like old leather, and its backbone is sticking out. The lower part of the body seems to be still frozen into the ice. It doesn't have any hair. There are signs of clothing and other items close to the body.

This same year, five or six other bodies have already been found in the mountains, as the summer sun melts the thinnest areas of ice. Often, they are the bodies of climbers who have fallen to their deaths down cracks in the ice. Some have been missing for as long as fifty years.

The first officials on the scene quickly realise that this is not a recent body, but has been in the ice a lot longer. They ask local scientists to come and take a look.

Whose body is it?

How did it get here?

What happens next?

The body has been **preserved** (kept intact) for hundreds of years because it was frozen inside a massive block of ice. Being out in the sun will soon make it to start to rot. It needs to be freed quickly.

Ski-poles, ice axes and drills are used. They are not ideal because they can damage the body, but there is no time to lose.

The body is taken to a nearby university, and placed in a deep freeze to stop it rotting further from contact with the air.

Over the next few months, scientists confirm the body is that of a man. But they make a much more surprising discovery. This man is over *five thousand years old!*

Amazingly, his body has survived in the ice since the **Neolithic period** or "new" Stone Age. The first clue comes from his copper axe, which is dated by an expert. This date is then confirmed by measuring the age of his bones.

A fully-clothed man from this long ago, with his belongings, has never been found before.

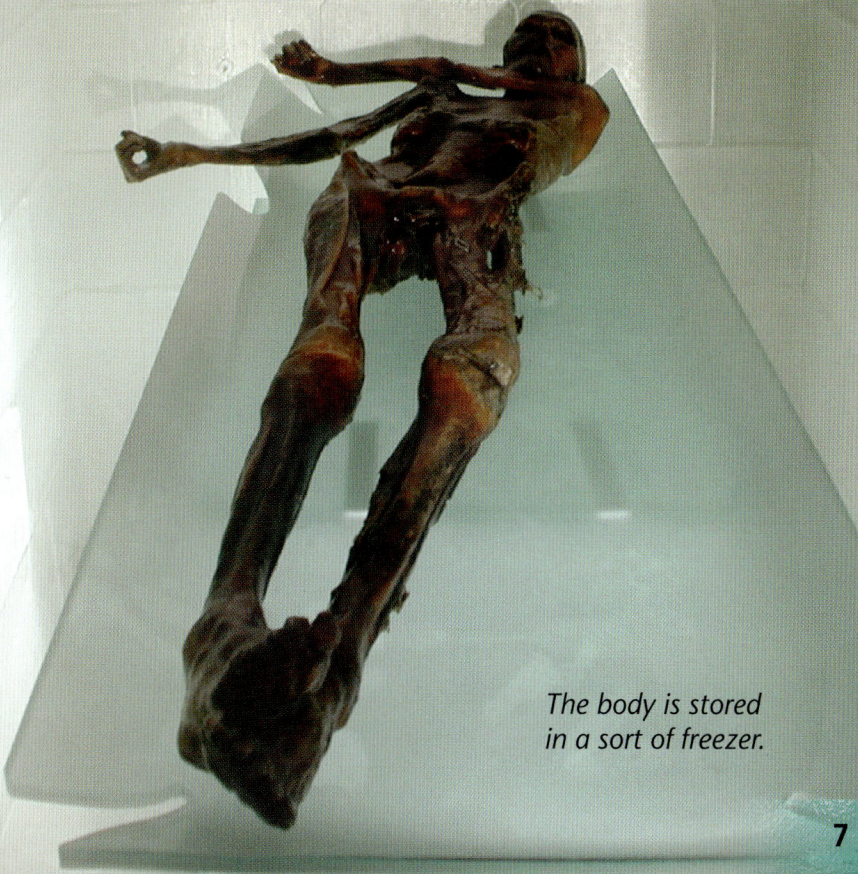

The body is stored in a sort of freezer.

One of the first tasks is to try to find out the cause of death.

The scientists carefully open up the body in a process called an **autopsy**. The Ice Man's skin is peeled back so scientists can see the state of his organs and identify the contents of his stomach.

By measuring his leg bones, scientists work out that he would have been around five feet two inches in height. They also discover that he has several injuries, including fractured ribs. These could have been caused by a fall, or perhaps by the pressure of the ice on top of his body.

The scientists call the Ice Man "Ötzi", after the area of the Ötztal Alps where he was found.

> **How to say his name**
> Ötzi is said aloud as "ert-zee".

As more scientists get to work, they begin to piece together the story of what might have happened to Ötzi.

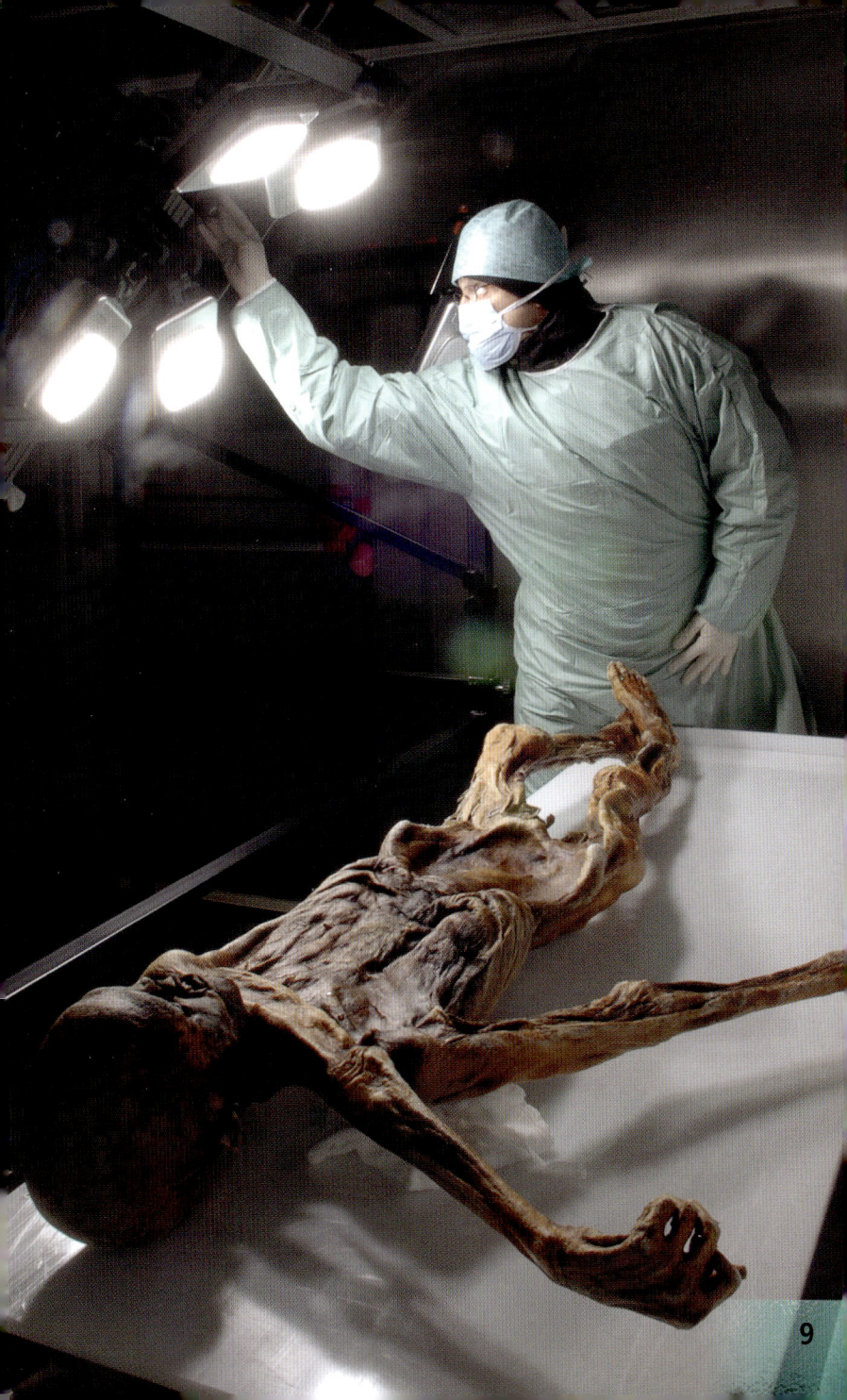

Studying the Ice Man

Ötzi's body is brought out from storage many times to be examined by scientists. Different scientists are interested in different things. Sometimes they are interested in a particular part of his body, sometimes a piece of his equipment.

They scan and photograph him in all possible ways, and poke and prod his bones and body. Books are printed, scientific reports written, and the facts about Ötzi are revealed like the pages of a book being turned, one by one.

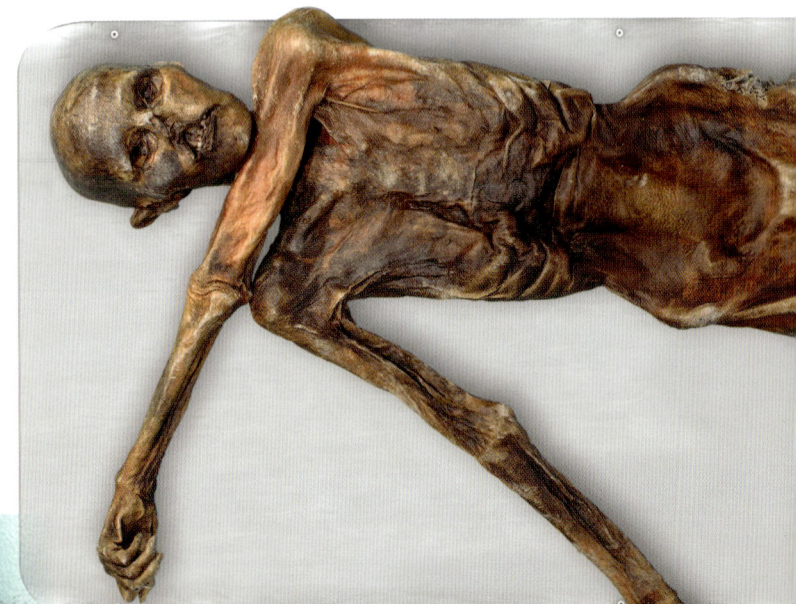

Here are some of the questions scientists hope to answer:

- What was he carrying and wearing?
- What was he doing so high in the mountains on that day?
- What did he eat?
- Where did he live?
- Was he a hunter or a farmer?

Turn the page now to find out more about Ötzi.

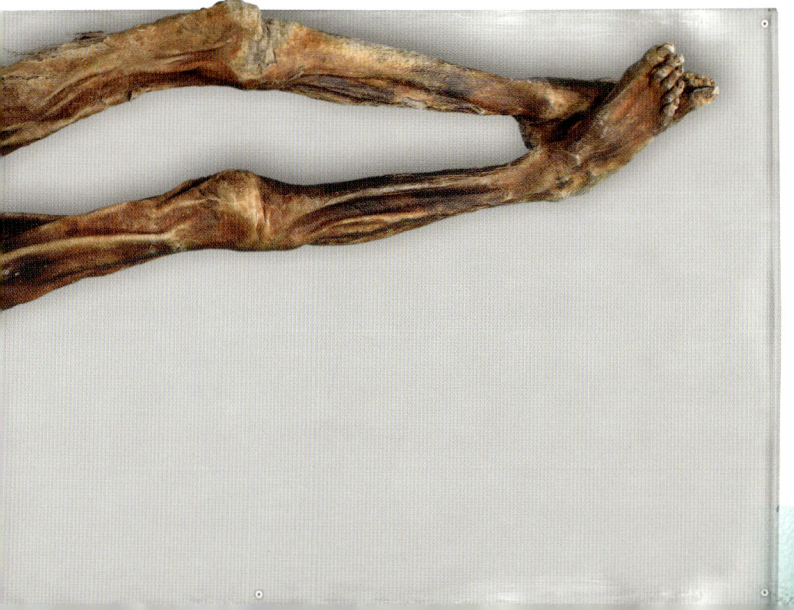

Body scan

A 3D scan of Ötzi's body is done using the latest technology.

Special cameras zoom in on his skin, which looks like wrinkled paper. They reveal its surface in great detail.

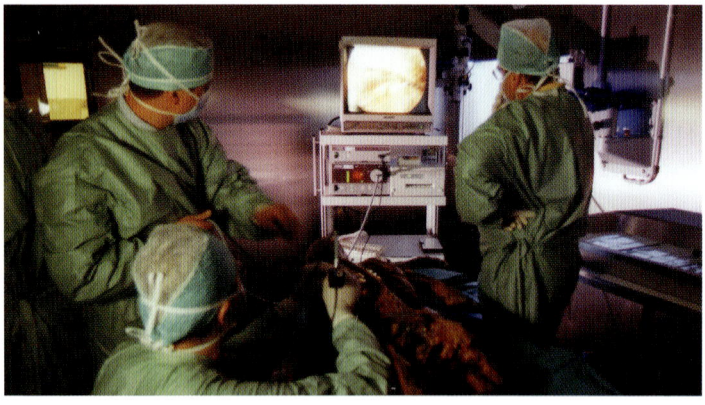

The scientists use **carbon dating** to reveal that he lived between 3350 and 3100 BC.

carbon dating
Carbon is a mineral found in all organic matter. Scientists can analyse the carbon to work out how old something is, even if it is many thousands of years old.

Detailed X-rays of the body reveal more hidden secrets. As well as finding broken bones, the X-rays show that a stone arrowhead is stuck in Ötzi's shoulder, where he has a large wound. Was this the cause of his death?

Other injuries show he was involved in hand-to-hand fighting shortly before his death.

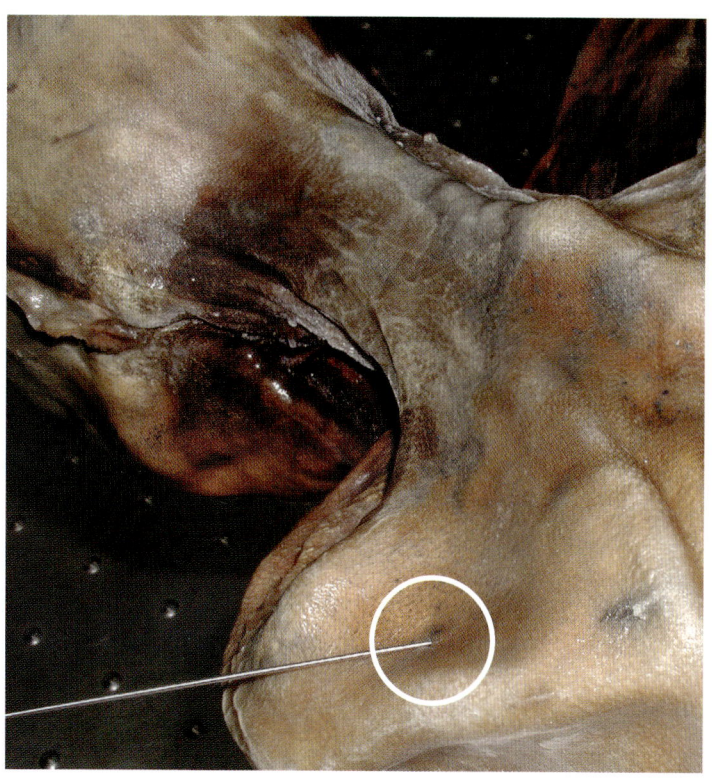

How old was the Ice Man?

The state of Ötzi's teeth and of his bone joints suggest he was around 45 years of age when he died. That was quite old for a man at the time.

The state of the teeth and bones provides very important evidence for **archaeologists**. The teeth and bones give a lot of information to help in working out how old a body is.

archaeologists
scientists who study the material remains of the past (bodies, objects, sites)

As we get older, our skeleton begins to show its age; we get aches and pains and may need to have some joints replaced. At 45, Ötzi would have been older than most other people alive at the time.

Is his age important?

Because Ötzi was probably older than most people in his community, he may have been seen as important, or wise. Some scientists have suggested that he may even have been deliberately buried after his death because so many important objects were found with him.

Today, a man living in the same area as Ötzi would expect to live for about 77 years. This is known as his **life expectancy**. Over time, people's life expectancies have risen because of better health care, and changes in our lifestyle.

At the time Ötzi was alive, his life expectancy would probably have been less than 30 years.

Ötzi's tattoos

Ötzi had over fifty tattoos, including a series of lines on either side of his spine. He also had a cross-shaped tattoo on one knee. The tattoos are all groups of lines and crosses.

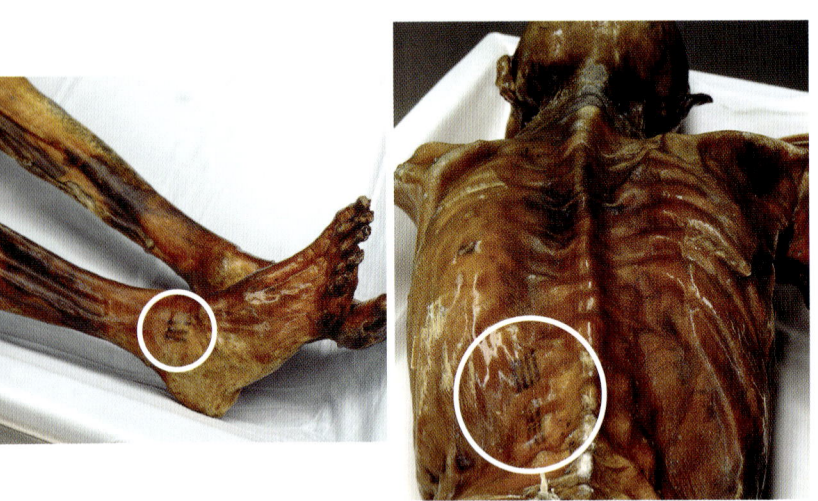

Why did Ötzi have tattoos?

Perhaps the tattoos marked an event or were a sign of Ötzi's membership of a group. Perhaps they were even done as part of a ceremony at a certain age, to prove that he could stand pain or was ready to be a man.

Because of the location of the tattoos, many scientists believe they were done for pain relief.

We will never know the real secret of Ötzi's tattoos.

How were the tattoos made?

The tattoos were made by piercing the skin with a bone needle or long thorns. Ötzi had a bone needle in his belongings. Soot from the fire was then rubbed into the open wounds. Shiny pieces of quartz were found in them too.

The tattoos would have taken many days to create, but Ötzi didn't show them off. They were in places that were hidden by clothing, so they weren't for display, as many tattoos today are.

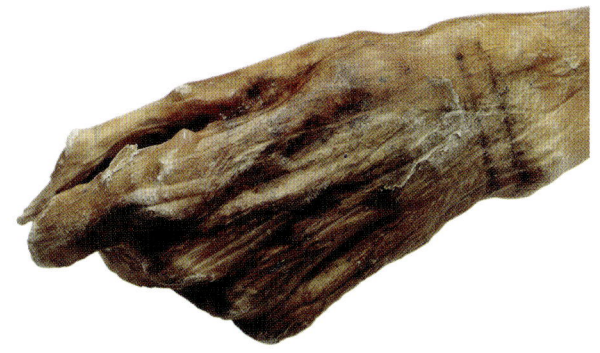

Was he healthy?

When scientists look at the contents of Ötzi's stomach, they find he had a worm living in his belly. That would have been painful. He had bone problems, too, and would have had pain in his joints as he made his way up into the mountains. This suggests that he had to climb for a reason, rather than for fun.

We would certainly notice these problems if we had them ourselves, but in Ötzi's time there were no doctors with the skill to treat them.

Even without the dental care and toothpaste that we have today, Ötzi's teeth were quite free of cavities. They were worn down and damaged, though. Imagine having no chance to see a dentist if your teeth hurt.

Another interesting discovery is that he was carrying pieces of a fungus that grows on birch trees. This fungus helps to keep wounds free from germs and can even help treat a stomach worm. Was Ötzi carrying a Stone Age first-aid kit with him?

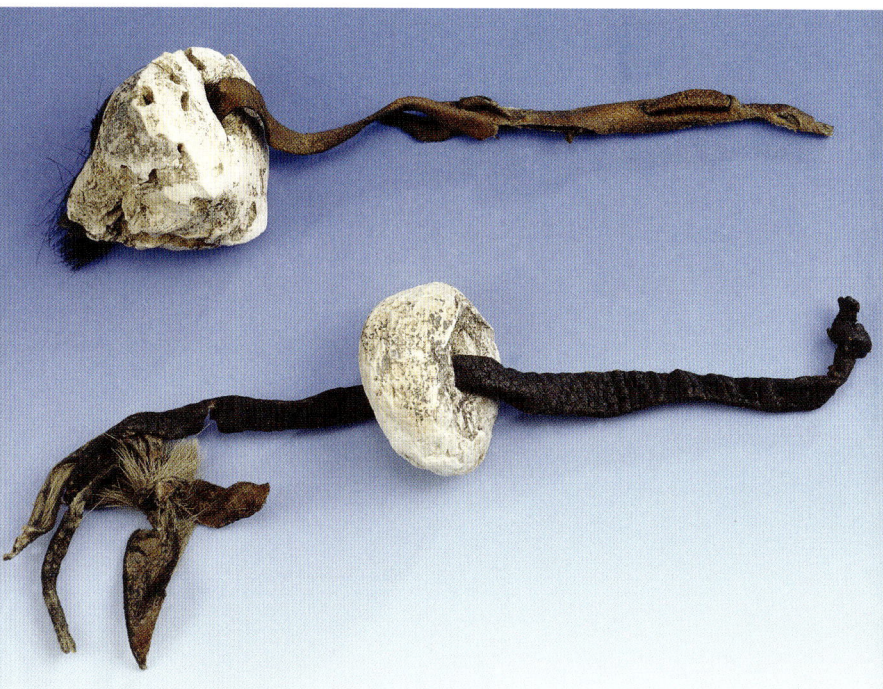

Was this part of Ötzi's first-aid kit?

Goat sandwich, anyone?

Scientists feed a camera on a long tube into Ötzi's stomach so they can see what he'd had for lunch 5000 years ago.

They discover that his last meal was ibex, a type of mountain goat, and red deer. The cooked meat was eaten with bread baked from wheat. This suggests that Ötzi lived down in the valley where crops were grown or that he had access to wild grains, which were ground into flour and baked. Baking would have been the job of someone in a larger community of people.

Ötzi's diet was fairly healthy, although his last meal didn't include many vegetables. He did at least eat an apple for one of his five a day!

There were some wild foods like nuts and berries in his stomach, too. Ötzi might have gathered these to eat, but they certainly weren't common in the high mountains where he was found. Perhaps family members picked them amongst the meadows in the valley?

The latest fashion?

Modern climbers wear strong, waterproof boots to keep out the cold and damp, along with windproof clothing and fleece layers. Ötzi didn't have any of these modern fabrics. He would also have had to rely on his own sense of direction, rather than a compass or GPS handset. His only map would have been in his head.

Ötzi's boots were made from leather, as were his leggings. His boots were stuffed with grass. He was wearing a fur hat to keep the cold out, a wrap, and a cape made from woven grass.

Even in the summer months, the temperature is cold when you are high up in the mountains. For every one hundred metres that you climb, it gets one degree cooler. Ötzi's body was found at a height of several thousand metres. As Ötzi climbed, he would become warm with the effort, but he would need his hide coat and bearskin cap when he stopped for a rest.

You would expect a hunter to have worn clothes made from animals that were shot or trapped. Some of Ötzi's clothing was made from sheep's wool, so was he a shepherd rather than a hunter? Perhaps this trip up into the mountains was unusual. Was he chased and attacked by other hunters? Was this where he received his arrow wound? During the new Stone Age, humans began to settle in one place, and started to grow crops and keep animals for their food.

Around his waist was a belt. Dangling from the belt was a pouch which contained some small items made from flint, a bone needle and a mossy plant that could be used to start fires.

What can Ötzi's belongings tell us?

Ötzi had a number of weapons.

He carried a longbow with a supply of arrows, a stone knife and a box made from birch bark. This was too small for arrows, but was possibly used to carry things to help him light a fire.

26

The most important tool he carried with him was a copper-bladed axe, with a shaft about two feet long. It showed signs of being used, and the fact that Ötzi owned such an item tells us he was probably an important man.

He probably made his own tools, perhaps with the help of his father, or some skilled person within the community.

Each arrow was made by hand. Ötzi would have carefully cut and smoothed the wood that made each arrow shaft, patiently created the sharp stone heads, and shaped the flights that helped the arrows fly straight and true.

Ötzi's last day...

It is a cloudy and windswept day in September. A bearded man picks his way carefully through the loose piles of stones that litter the slopes of a high snow-capped mountain peak. He is in a hurry, and he is in pain.

He has blood escaping from a shoulder wound. He has pressed moss to the wound to try to stop the bleeding, but it is not working very well. He gasps with each footstep but he can't clutch his side as he is carrying a longbow and other tools. He crosses the mountain pass to where he can start going down.

He looks back up at the jagged heights of the peak and starts downhill. The weather is changing for the worse. In the mountains, the weather changes quickly. Clouds are building from the west, and as he looks down at the valley where his family and friends are waiting, the view is blocked by a sudden shower of icy hail.

He decides to take shelter in a gully, as snow begins to fall on his fur hat and the fur wrap around his shoulders. He lifts the moss away from the wound, but it is too painful to touch and is still bleeding heavily. He listens. Is he still being chased?

He carefully lays his copper axe to one side – it is his most important tool. He could light a fire, but there is nothing to burn up here. If he can just sleep for a while, perhaps he can move on when the weather gets better.

He nibbles on some cold meat and a husk of wheat bread. He cups his hands, which are streaked with blood, and sips some of the ice cold water that is trickling past his feet.

He closes his eyes, wrapping his cape around him. The snow keeps falling … the first sign that winter is coming.

His eyes close, for the last time …

An icy grave

As those first winter snows cloak Ötzi's body, water begins to soak into his clothes and form in pools beneath his body. Layers of snow fall on top of him, and by the start of the following year, he is buried beneath several metres of snow.

Each summer, as the top layers of snow melt, water soaks down, then refreezes.

Over time, the weight of the snow squeezes the air out of the snow, turning it into hard ice. The cold temperatures suck the water out of Ötzi's body, turning him into an ice mummy. His body is also squeezed by the pressure of the ice, and some of his belongings rot away.

As Ötzi lies in his icy tomb, the years, decades, centuries tick away. The cold temperatures preserve Ötzi's body, and his skin turns brown, like leather. Further snow builds on top of him and ensures that he is not found in a hurry.

Ötzi misses out on a great deal:

- the birth and founding of religions
- global conflicts
- great scientific discoveries.

Seasons come and go, and decades and centuries pass.

As the years go by, the climate slowly warms. Less snow falls than before, and some of the ice retreats.

Slowly the landscape becomes settled, people farm the land, and swarm over it in horses and carts, then cars, lorries and trucks.

Instead of fearing the mountains, the people begin to make their living from them. Tourists start visiting the area – people like the Simons who discovered the body of Ötzi on one such trip.

The climate changes even more and the warmth finally reaches down through the ice towards Ötzi. It begins to reveal him for the first time in thousands of years, until at last he feels the September sun on his back.

Bringing him (and us) back to the 21st century …

Mountain scenery

Would Ötzi recognise the Alps of today?

The ice that Ötzi was buried in was part of a **glacier**. There are many glaciers in the Alps. Glaciers are often described as "rivers of ice". Time lapse photography shows that they move very slowly downhill. The weight of the ice pressing down on the bottom layers makes them move like plasticine pushed down by a hand.

As they flow, they shape the landscape and create deep, steep-sided valleys.

This valley in Scotland, Glen Coe, was formed by a glacier.

Although mountains may look the same from year to year, they are slowly being changed. As well as the glaciers, the changes are made by the processes of **weathering**. The regular daily change from the heat of the sun to the frosts at night finally weakens even the hardest rocks. Winter storms, combined with frost, running water and lightning strikes, shatter them. This produces loose rocks, which pile up into slopes called **screes**. Large rock-falls can happen at any time.

The Alps attract many visitors, and not all of them return home safely. Even today, there are deaths each year through accidents. Mountains must be treated with respect. Ötzi would have known that too, and perhaps feared them as places where dangerous creatures lived.

This glacier in Argentina is moving slowly between the mountains.

What are avalanches?

An **avalanche** is a massive amount of snow crashing down the mountain. In winter, avalanches of snow regularly sweep down the steep slopes in the Alps. Snow falls heavily, and piles up along mountain ridges and peaks where wind swirls around them.

Avalanches can sometimes be set off by noises, and in the past they have even been used as weapons. During the Second World War, avalanches were started on purpose to try to kill German troops. More often, they are caused by snow building up until it collapses under its own weight, particularly when temperatures warm up.

Avalanches can travel at speeds of over 200 miles per hour. They push a shockwave ahead of them, which can damage the forests on the slopes. This in turn makes future avalanches more likely.

People trapped in the snow are quickly unable to breathe. Modern climbers or skiers often carry a transmitter that will be triggered by an avalanche. Rescue teams use trained dogs and long probes, and must work quickly. Hundreds of people are buried in the snow every year, although usually for much less time than Ötzi.

Ötzi would perhaps have stared in wonder at avalanches on the other side of the valley, and heard the roar of the snow, wondering at the forces of nature that created them.

More bodies

Ötzi is not the only person to have been found preserved in the ground.

Tollund Man

The body of Tollund Man was found in a peat bog in central Denmark in 1950. Two brothers were digging peat for fuel. A young man had gone missing a few days earlier, and, as they dug through the soft peat, they came across the body of a man with a rope round his neck.

The brothers called the police, who treated it as a crime scene – the body had been so well preserved in the peat that they thought it had not been there for long. Further study showed that this man had actually lived in the Iron Age, about 2400 years ago.

Strangely, the body of another man and a woman were later found in the same area. They are thought to be from the Iron Age, too, and also appeared to have been murdered. The woman had been hanged and the man's neck had been slit from ear to ear.

The **acidic** peat had kept all these bodies preserved, by shutting out the air that would have rotted them. They are now displayed in a museum, and the scientists have carried out similar work on their bodies to uncover their secrets.

Ice mummies

In 1845, the explorer Sir John Franklin set off on a British **expedition** to the Arctic in two ships. His aim was to find a shipping route through the ice from the north of Canada to Asia. This route was called the Northwest Passage, and Franklin was one of several men who tried to find the route. It would be a valuable discovery for Britain at the time.

But the ships disappeared, along with their crew of 128 men.

During the first year, the ships became frozen in the ice in the north of Canada. Franklin thought he was ready for this, and had taken supplies of tinned food: a new idea at the time. However, the ships remained stuck in the ice for two years!

Franklin died and the remaining men decided to try to walk to safety. Not a single person made it back.

Other expeditions set out to try to find the ships, but they were unsuccessful. Over the years, some of the crew's bodies have been discovered, as well as items from the ships.

In the 1980s, a group of modern explorers dug up three crew members frozen into the coffins in which they had been placed over 120 years earlier. The ground in the Arctic is called **permafrost** and had acted like a deep freeze. The crew members were almost unchanged and their eyes stared up when their icy tombs were opened. An autopsy revealed high levels of lead in their bodies. It is thought the tins their food had been kept in poisoned them.

The two ships that Franklin sailed in have never been found.

45

So what of Ötzi now?

Today, the Ötztal area of the Alps is more popular with tourists as a result of Ötzi's discovery. Many visitors make the journey up to the area where Ötzi's body was found. A pillar made from local stones marks the point where he was discovered.

Visitors stand by the memorial and think back through the centuries.

There is a museum for visitors who want to find out more about Ötzi and the work of the scientists studying him.

Ötzi's body is kept in safe storage and is not usually displayed. But the museum has something just as exciting: a model of Ötzi as he may have looked.

His skull gave scientists clues to how his face would have looked. They were able to look at his bones and work out how his muscles and flesh would have sat on them and, from this, how his face would have appeared. Add some hair and you can recreate the Ice Man's face.

Measurements of his bones allowed his body to be recreated too.

Imagine coming face-to-face with the Ice Man. Now you can. Turn the page to see him.

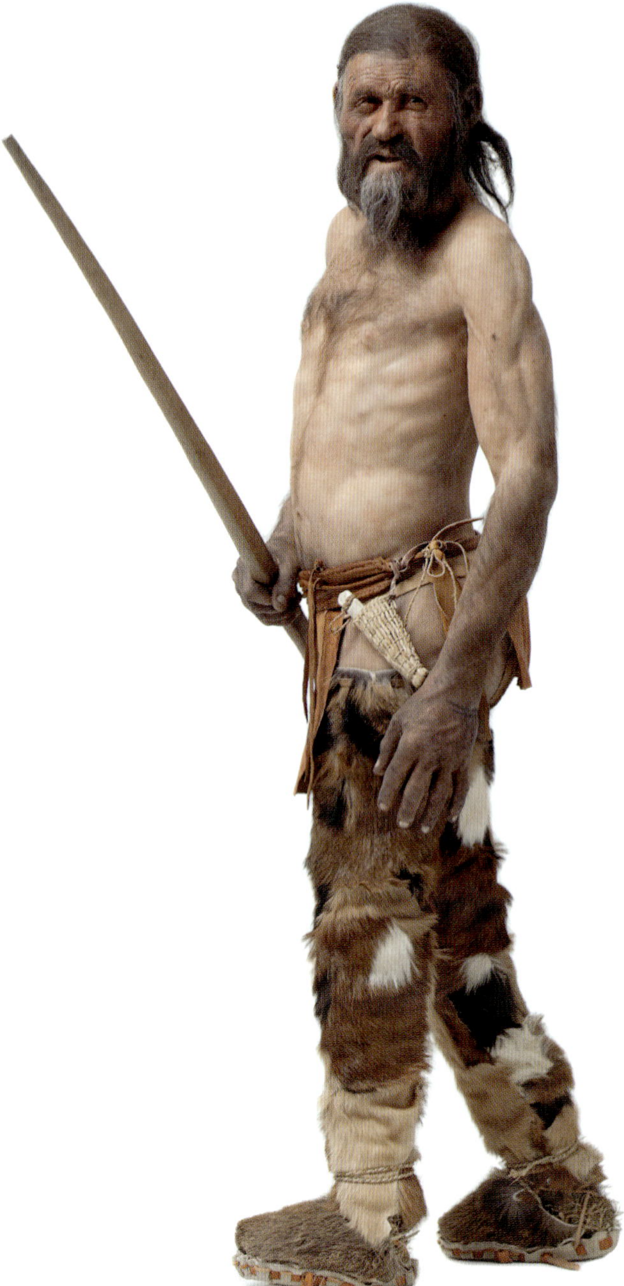

Does Ötzi look as you expected? And how can we know what he looked like?

It is likely that he would not have been clean shaven. Shaving takes effort and the long hair would also have helped keep him warm. It would probably have been streaked with grey. His was not an easy life.

Imagine that you could talk to Ötzi. What would you want to ask him?

- Did you have any children?
- Why were you up in the mountains? Were you lost?
- The weather in the mountains can change quickly. Were you taking shelter from a sudden winter storm?

In some ways, Ötzi will live forever. He is a time traveller who is still here, 5300 years after he was born …

CSI Ötzi

Advances in science are helping to uncover more of Ötzi's secrets. One of these is DNA analysis.

DNA is part of the cells that make up our bodies. It contains coded information which decides whether we have blue or brown eyes, for example.

In recent years, DNA analysis has become more important in crime cases. Even one hair at a crime scene can be matched to a person and prove that he or she was there.

Scientists worked on Ötzi's DNA but, because he was so old, it took them *two years* to piece it together and even longer to make sense of what it told them. In fact it was only in 2012 that they completed this work – over twenty years after the discovery of his body.

This allowed them to say that he had brown eyes. They found out that he had an allergy to milk, and that he had blood type O.

The work continues. There are more secrets to uncover.

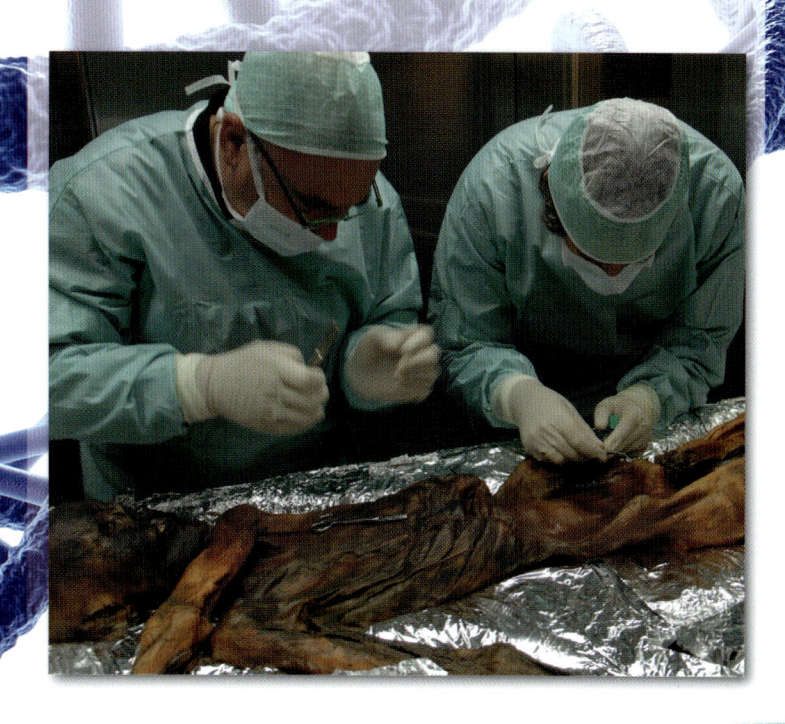

Reader challenge

Word hunt

1. On page 8, find an adjective that means "broken".

2. On page 18, find a noun that means "holes formed by decay".

3. On page 29, find an adjective that means "pointed and uneven".

Text sense

4. Using the text on page 36, describe how a glacier forms.

5. Give two examples of other bodies that have been preserved for many years. (pages 40–45)

6. Why do you think visitors like to visit Ötzi's memorial? (page 46)

7. How did scientists work out what Ötzi would have looked like? (pages 48–49)

8. Why do you think it is important for scientists to find out about Ötzi and what his life was like?

Your views

9. How close to the truth about Ötzi do you think scientists can get in their work? Give reasons.

10. What other secrets about Ötzi do you think scientists might uncover in the future?

Spell it

With a partner, look at these words and then cover them up.

- scene (as in: "A body was found at the scene.")
- muscle (as in: "a muscle in your body")
- scientist

Take it in turns for one of you to read the words aloud. The other person has to try and spell each word. Check your answers, then swap over.

Try it

Read page 51 again. With a partner, imagine one of you is Ötzi and the other is a scientist interested in finding out more about the Ice Man's life. As the scientist, think of five different questions to ask Ötzi. Ötzi must answer the questions, using information learned from the text.

William Collins's dream of knowledge for all began with the publication of his first book in 1819. A self-educated mill worker, he not only enriched millions of lives, but also founded a flourishing publishing house. Today, staying true to this spirit, Collins books are packed with inspiration, innovation and practical expertise. They place you at the centre of a world of possibility and give you exactly what you need to explore it.

Collins. Freedom to teach.

Published by Collins Education
An imprint of HarperCollins*Publishers*
77–85 Fulham Palace Road, Hammersmith, London W6 8JB

Browse the complete Collins Education catalogue at **www.collinseducation.com**

Text by Alan Parkinson
© HarperCollins*Publishers* Limited 2012
Illustrations by Stewart Johnson
© HarperCollins*Publishers* Limited 2012

Series consultants: Alan Gibbons and Natalie Packer

10 9 8 7 6 5 4 3 2 1
ISBN 978-0-00-748477-5

All rights reserved. No part of this publication may be reproduced, stored in a retrieval system, or transmitted in any form or by any means, electronic, mechanical, photocopying, recording or otherwise, without the prior written permission of the Publisher or a licence permitting restricted copying in the United Kingdom issued by the Copyright Licensing Agency Ltd, 90 Tottenham Court Road, London W1T 4LP.

British Library Cataloguing in Publication Data.
A catalogue record for this publication is available from the British Library.

Commissioned by Catherine Martin
Edited and project-managed by Sue Chapple
Picture research and proofreading by Grace Glendinning
Illustration management by Tim Satterthwaite
Design and typesetting by Jordan Publishing Design Limited
Cover design by Paul Manning

Acknowledgements

The publishers would like to thank the students and teachers of the following schools for their help in trialling the Read On series:

Southfields Academy, London
Queensbury School, Queensbury, Bradford
Langham C of E Primary School, Langham, Rutland
Ratton School, Eastbourne, East Sussex
Northfleet School for Girls, North Fleet, Kent
Westergate Community School, Chichester, West Sussex
Bottesford C of E Primary School, Bottesford, Nottinghamshire
Woodfield Academy, Redditch, Worcestershire
St Richard's Catholic College, Bexhill, East Sussex

The publishers gratefully acknowledge the permission granted to reproduce the copyright material in this book. While every effort has been made to trace and contact copyright holders, where this has not been possible the publishers will be pleased to make the necessary arrangements at the first opportunity.

The publisher would like to thank the following for permission to reproduce pictures in these pages (t = top, b = bottom, c = centre, l = left, r = right):

p 3 Austrian Police, p 5 Vienna Report Agency/Sygma/Corbis, pp 20–21 Roca/Shutterstock, p 22t Daniele Silva/Shutterstock, p 22cl dspring/Shutterstock, p 22bl Przemyslaw Ceynowa/Shutterstock, p 23tl Karkas/Shutterstock, p 23cl dspring/Shutterstock, p 24l dspring/Shutterstock, p 25t bogdan ionescu/Shutterstock, p 36 Nella/Shutterstock, pp 36–37 Pablo H Caridad/Shutterstock, p 39 StockShot/Alamy, p 40 Robin Weaver/Alamy, p 41 Christina Gascoigne/Getty Images, pp 42–43 © Look and Learn/Bridgeman, p 45 Owen Beattie/University of Alberta, pp 52–53 dencg/Shutterstock.

The following images have been provided courtesy of the South Tyrol Museum of Archaeology, Bolzano, South Tyrol, Italy:

pp 2–3, pp 4–5, p 7, p 12, p 13, p 14, pp 16–17, p 19, p 22cr, 22br, p 23tr, 23cr, p 24r, p 25b, pp 26–27, p 46, p 47: South Tyrol Museum of Archaeology

p 9 South Tyrol Museum of Archaeology/Eurac/Samadelli/Staschitz, pp 10–11 South Tyrol Museum of Archaeology/Eurac/Samadelli/Staschitz, pp 34–35 South Tyrol Museum of Archaeology/photo Robert Clark, pp 48–49 South Tyrol Museum of Archaeology/A. Ochsenreiter (reconstruction), South Tyrol Museum of Archaeology/Heike Engel-21 Lux, p 50 South Tyrol Museum of Archaeology/A. Ochsenreiter (reconstruction), South Tyrol Museum of Archaeology/Heike Engel-21 Lux, p 53 South Tyrol Museum of Archaeology/Eurac/Samadelli.